penny

Jeffrey Patnaude

ILLUSTRATIONS BY DON VIERSTRA

Published by White Rhino Press
319-J S. Westgate Drive
Greensboro, NC   27407
877-643-1303

Publisher's Cataloging-in-Publication Data
Patnaude, Jeffrey.
      Penny / by Jeffrey Patnaude;
      Illustrations by Don Vierstra
      —Greensboro, NC : White Rhino Press, 2003.

            p. ; cm.

            ISBN 0-9704122-2-3
            1. Counting—Juvenile literature.
            I. Vierstra, Don.

QA113 .P38 2003
513.2/11[E] —dc21   0306

Project coordination by Jenkins Group, Inc. • www.bookpublishing.com
Illustrated by Don Vierstra
Book design by Kelli Leader

07 06 05 04 03 * 5 4 3 2 1

Printed in China

This book is dedicated to

President Abraham Lincoln.

Still making a difference....

This story begins on a path far away, where Penny was stuck in a place where it stayed,

r year after year, until it finally found,

a way from the roadside, a way into town.

Picked up by a traveler, **1** Penny I'll own.

HOURS

AM-6PM

AM-4 PM

CLOSED

Then into her pocket,
no longer alone.

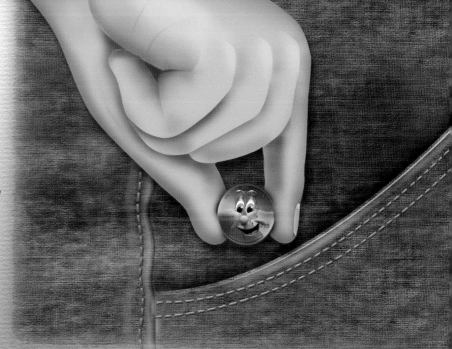

For down in the dark, was another small coin,

a penny from elsewhere,
now **2** of them joined.

"Hello," said the penny, "I'm here from the ground."
The other was happy that Penny was found.

For pennies together make music you see.

But jingles from 2 cents are better from 3.

Number **3** came from nowhere - right out of the sky. Inside a balloon from a party nearby?

So into the pocket, with the other 2
they happily jingled, 'cause that's what they do.

The traveler now had **3** whole pennies to spend,
but 4 would be more, if she could just add a friend.

While looking around her she opened a door, and there was another; it was number 4.

4 pennies are **4** coins; **2** pennies plus **2**.
They jingled so loudly, she knew what she'd do.

She let out a laugh 'cause she had such a tickle. "I'll find one more penny, and make them a nickel."

"No!" said the pennies, "We like who we are. Just find us another and we'll make you a star."

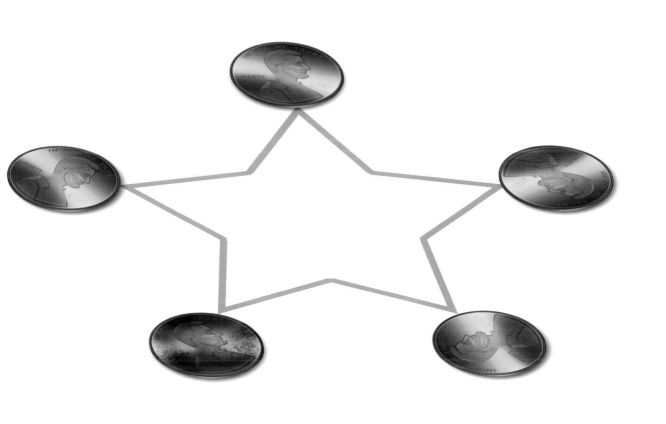

So find one she did, and then placed them around

5 points of a star, as she lay each one down.

The traveler walked on, "No more pennies for me. 1 nickel is easier to carry you see."

But stars can be helpful to search and discover.
The light from the star shone to find them another.

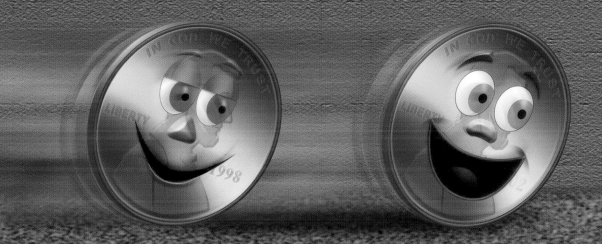

Just then, in rolled **7**, then followed by **8**.
2 pennies at once, that's because they were mates.

8 pennies together can stack up quite tall,
so they decided to do so, to see past a wall.

Penny was first, then 2, 3, 4, 5, 6.
Mates 7 and 8 jumped on. Oh what a trick!

8 said, "I see one, it's way out on the street. We'll roll out and get it, use our edges as feet."

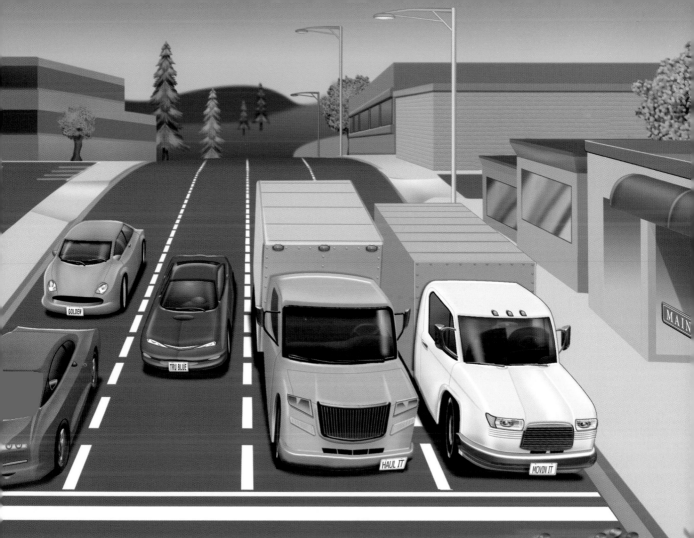

So they rolled past **3** cars, **2** big trucks and **1**
sign. To the roll add another, and now they were **9**.

Now **9** is just fine, it's only **3**, **3**, and **3**,

or **5** plus **4** more,

or **8** and **1** Penny.

But **10** is far different from pennies of **9**.
To add **1** to **9** is the same as a dime.

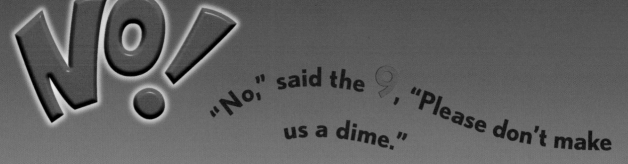

"No," said the 9, "Please don't make us a dime."

Each penny's important, each 1 that you find.

For where would we be without 2 cents or 1?

We make a small difference, but we're having fun.

So the pennies continued to find more and more. They stacked, and they rolled, and made stars on the floor.

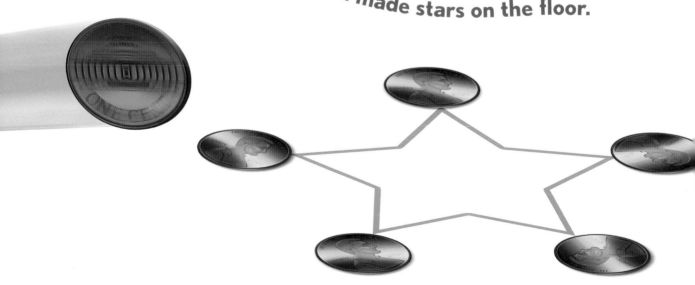

They happily jingled, not as nickels or dimes. They were pennies forever, meant to last a long time.

The End
No!
It's the beginning!

You now can follow a pathway of your own,
by finding lost pennies and bringing them home.

Put one in each slot as you count 1 to 10.
When done, you can start up all over again.

Find number one and push penny in by the nose.
Then you'll find 2, you know how it goes.

Take 10 pennies to stop, give away or make change,
and don't be discouraged if you get looks that are strange.

For you have a mission for finding pennies so lost.
Go out and get them and don't let them be tossed.

For making a difference is what we all do,
and the world just may need one small gift made by you!

We invite you to share your stories with us.
As your children start to save,
let us know about the many different choices
they make concerning what to do with their saved pennies.
Send your stories to us via the U.S. Postal Service
or by e-mail to penny@patnaude.com.

In one of the future books,
we will share these stories for all to enjoy.

Look for these upcoming books and CD's from

Livonia - The Lady of the Shadows
Oak & Maple
Tex & Jiffie
The Adventures of Herman Bean

White Rhino Press
319-J S. Westgate Drive
Greensboro, NC 27407
336-315-5363
Printed in China